11+ Maths

Standard Practice Paper
Pack Two 11A

Fill in your details:

Name..

Date of birth...

Male ☐   Female ☐

School..

Today's date...

Read these instructions before you start:

- You have **50 minutes** to complete this paper.
- There are **50 questions** in this paper and each question is worth one mark.
- Show all working using the space around the questions. You may receive marks for correct working even if your final answer is wrong.
- Make sure you write the answers very clearly.
- You will not lose marks for crossing out.
- Work as quickly and carefully as you can.
- If you find a question difficult, do **NOT** spend too much time on it but move on to the next one.
- **Calculators and protractors are not allowed.**

Moon Tuition
making the most of your potential

www.moontuition.co.uk

1   Work out $3785 + 849$

Answer:_____

2   Work out $1264 - 368$

Answer:_____

3   Work out 56×12

Answer:_____

4   Work out $6041 \div 7$

Answer:_____

5   Write down the number three hundred and one thousand four hundred and seven in figures.

Answer:_____

6   Write down eighteen and 4 tenths as a decimal.

Answer:_____

7   You are told: $16 \times 265 = 4240$
Work out 8×265

Answer:_____

8   Charlie thinks of a number. He adds five, then multiplies by three and then subtracts six. His answer is 30. What is the number that Charlie first thought of?

Answer:_____

9   Estimate the value of $399.8 \div 20.19$ and circle the correct answer.

200   20   2   100   15

10   John bought a Comic magazine costing £4.50 and 6 sweets costing 20p each.

How much change did he get from a £10 note?

Answer:_____

11   Arrange the following numbers in order, biggest first.

0.27   0.09   0.23   0.41   1.35

Answer:_____

12   Work out 50×400

Answer:_____

13 Work out 2.436×100

Answer:_____

---

14 Which of the following numbers below, when divided by 3 gives a whole number between 10 and 20?

13   84   46   54   75

Answer:_____

---

15 Each box holds a dozen eggs. How many eggs are there in total if there are 8 boxes?

Answer:_____

---

16 What is the next number in the pattern?

144   121   100   81   _____

Answer:_____

---

17 There are 36 students in Year 5 class. They are be divided into two teams for an activity so that team A has twice as many students as team B. How many students are there in team A?

Answer:_____

18   What is $\frac{2}{3}$ of 120?

Answer:_____

19   Lucy has £2 pocket money, how many chocolate bars costing 45p each can she buy?

Answer:_____

20   Tom needs to prepare for his violin recital this week. He will perform three violin pieces in the concert. He needs to practise 10 minutes for each piece every day. How many hours in total does he need to practise for the whole week including the weekend?

Answer:_____

21

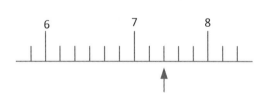

What is the number indicated by the arrow?

Answer:_____

22   Two civil engineers can complete a task within 6 days. How long will it take 3 civil engineers to complete the same task?

Answer:_____

23   There are 56 people in the room. How many do you think were born on a Wednesday?

Answer:_____

24   Jonathan weighs 46.5*kg* and Marcus is 2.7*kg* lighter than Jonathan. How heavy is Marcus?

Answer:_____

25   Find 75% of £200.

Answer:_____

26

10cm

5cm

2cm

Not to scale

4cm

What is the perimeter of this shape?

Answer:_____

27   A TV costs £800. There is 20% off in the Christmas sale. What is the sale price?

Answer:_____

28   There are 3 green, 8 red, 5 yellow and 4 blue balloons. What is the probability of picking a yellow balloon?

Answer:_____

29 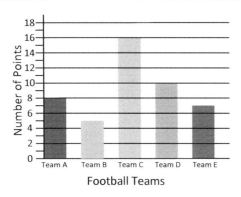 This graph shows 5 football teams' match results for last month. What is the range of the match results?

Answer:_____

30 $x - 30 = 49$. What is x?

Answer:_____

31   There are 450 children in school. $\frac{3}{5}$ of them will go on a school trip to London. How many children will **not** go on the school trip?

Answer:_____

32   What is the nearest number to 2000 you can make from the digits 3 9 1 8?

Answer:_____

33   You are told: $45 \times 246 = 11070$
Use this result to work out 4.5×24.6

Answer:_____

34   You are told: 3^4 is $3 \times 3 \times 3 \times 3$, which gives the answer 81.
What is 2^4?

Answer:_____

35 $0.006km$ $708cm$ $7\frac{1}{4}m$ $6.3m$ $3894mm$

Place the above measurements in order, starting with the smallest and ending with the biggest. Which one will be in the middle?

Answer:_____

36   Add together $2.4l$, $850ml$ and $400ml$. Give your answer in litres.

Answer:_____

37   What is the area of this shape?

Answer:_____

38   James wants to buy 4 burgers costing £3.98 each and 3 drinks costing 90p each. How much does he need to pay in total?

Answer:_____

39   Which of the following is the biggest? Circle the correct answer.

A) 80.9%   B) $\frac{2}{5}$ C) 82%   D) $\frac{3}{4}$ E) 0.8

40

	Train 1	Train 2
Reading	0710	1030
Maidenhead	0722	1044
London	0743	1109

How much shorter is the journey time of train 1 to travel from Reading to London than train 2?

Answer:_____

41   How many 8s do you need to type if you type all the numbers from 1 to 100?

Answer:_____

42   Jason's average cycling speed is $21km$ per hour. How far would he cycle in 2 hours and 20 minutes?

Answer:_____

43   A Maths teacher has 80 pencils, he gives out as many as he can to 12 children so that each gets the same number. How many does the teacher have left over?

Answer:_____

---

44   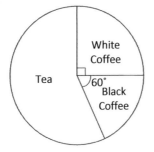   In a survey, 30 people like drinking black coffee, how many people like drinking tea ?

Answer:_____

---

45   Which one of the following numbers is a prime number?

21   35   2   51   33

Answer:_____

---

46   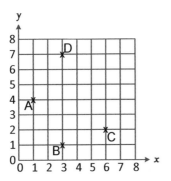   Write down the coordinates of point D.

Answer:_____

---

47   Edward bought 20 comic magazines for £4.99 each. He sold them for £6.49 each. How much profit did Edward make all together?

Answer:_____

48

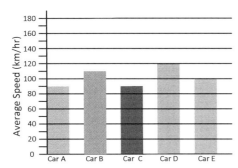

This graph shows the average speed of 5 different cars. What is the mean of the average speed?

Answer:_____

49   Paul pays £120 each month for his council tax. How much does he need to pay for a year?

Answer:_____

50   How many hundredths need to be added to 0.4 to make 0.7?

Answer:_____

11+ Maths

Standard Practice Paper
Pack Two 11B

Fill in your details:

Name...

Date of birth...

Male ☐   Female ☐

School..

Today's date...

Read these instructions before you start:

- You have **50 minutes** to complete this paper.
- There are **50 questions** in this paper and each question is worth one mark.
- Show all working using the space around the questions. You may receive marks for correct working even if your final answer is wrong.
- Make sure you write the answers very clearly.
- You will not lose marks for crossing out.
- Work as quickly and carefully as you can.
- If you find a question difficult, do **NOT** spend too much time on it but move on to the next one.
- **Calculators and protractors are not allowed.**

Moon Tuition
making the most of your potential

www.moontuition.co.uk

1 What is the missing number from the following calculation?

$$360 \div 12 = 6 \times \underline{\hspace{1cm}}$$

Answer:_____

2 What is the missing number in sequence below?

1, 1, 2, 6, 24, _____

Answer:_____

3

What is the number indicated by the arrow?

Answer:_____

4 Change 48% to a fraction. Leave your answer in its lowest term.

Answer:_____

5 The three numbers missing are all prime numbers. Write down these three numbers.

_____ × _____ × _____ = 555

Answer:_____

6

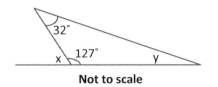

Not to scale

The left diagram shows a triangle. Work out the angles marked x and y.

Answer: x=_____;   y=_____

7

What is the missing number from the calculation below?

$(13+\underline{\hspace{2cm}}) \times 9 = 198$

Answer:_____

8

It was 7°C at noon in London. The temperature has dropped by 9°C. What is the temperature at midnight?

Answer:_____

9

Richard wants to buy 24 chocolate bars for his birthday party. A supermarket sells them at 25p for one chocolate bar, 40p for two chocolate bars and £1.50 for a pack of 10 chocolate bars. What is the smallest amount of money he needs to spend?

Answer:_____

10

Alex's height is 5 feet 8 inches. His friend Richard is 1.6 metres tall. Who is taller and by how many centimetres?

Answer:_____

---

11   Patrick wants to buy two books on sale. One is 20% off the original price £12 and the other one is 25% off the original price £16. How much does he need to pay for these two books?

Answer:_____

12   Find all the numbers that are multiple of 3.

      19   51   234   81   73   50

Answer:_____

13   Calculate 6.48×0.2 and round your answer to 2 decimal places.

Answer:_____

14   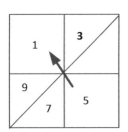   What is the probability of scoring a 9 on this spinner? Give your answer in percentage.

Answer:_____

15   Tom went to watch a film with his friends. It lasted 1 hour and 40 minutes. It finished at 4:25pm. When did the film start?

Answer:_____

© Moon Tuition
www.moontuition.co.uk

16   Round 43.9453 to the nearest hundredth.

Answer:_____

---

17   Bananas cost £1.60 per kilogram. How much would 300 grams cost?

Answer:_____

18

Not to Scale

What is the area of parallelogram ABCD?

Answer:_____

---

19   There are 240 boys in Dragon School. 80% of them are boarding. How many day boys are there?

Answer:_____

---

20   How many hundredths need to be added to 5.4 to make 6.3?

Answer:_____

---

21   James bought equal number of £1.20 magazines and £1.30 notebooks. He spent £10 in total. How many notebooks and magazines did he buy altogether?

Answer:_____

22 Add the smallest prime number greater than 20 to the biggest even number less than 100, you will get a square number. Is this statement TRUE or FALSE? Please show your working to prove your answer.

Answer:_____

23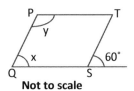
Not to scale

Calculate the angles x and y in parallelogram PQST?

Answer: x=_____;   y=_____

24 The flight from London to Orland took 9 hours. Lucy left at 7:30am. When she arrived there, the clock there said 10:30am. How many hours is Orland time behind London time?

Answer:_____

25 Write the following prices in order, starting with the biggest.
£8.60   £8.09   £9.06   96p   £0.99

Answer:_____

26 Which one of the following fractions is greater than 0.5 but less than 0.75?
$\frac{10}{25}$ $\frac{2}{8}$ $\frac{10}{16}$ $\frac{7}{8}$ $\frac{3}{4}$

Answer:_____

27

Desserts	
Ice Cream	£1.50
Apple Pie	£1.45
White Coffee	90p

A family spent £11 altogether on desserts. They ordered 3 ice creams, 2 apple pies and some white coffee. How many cups of white coffee did they order?

Answer:_____

28

IN	3	8	12	24	9
OUT	7	17	25		19

What is the missing number in this table?

Answer:_____

29

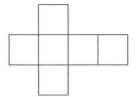

What 3-D shape does this net make?

Answer:_____

30

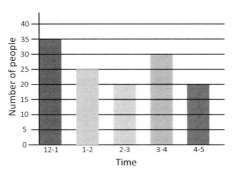

The bar chart shows the number of people visiting the post office on Friday afternoon. How many people visited between 1:00pm and 4pm?

Answer:_____

31

What percentage of this shape is not shaded?

Answer:_____

32

Kate has 3.2kg of flour. She needs $\frac{3}{8}$ of it to make cakes for her son's birthday party. How many kilograms does she need?

Answer:_____

33

Richard poured 2l apple juice into 4 bottles. The first one contained 0.75l, the second contained 800ml and the third one held 0.25l. How many litres did the fourth one hold?

Answer:_____

34

I think of a number, halve it and then subtract 6. I get $8\frac{1}{2}$. What number did I think of?

Answer:_____

35

Tom gets £3 pocket money per week for helping his mum with the house chores. He saves all his money towards a professional badminton racket which costs £135. How many weeks does it take him to save up for this badminton racket?

Answer:_____

36   Emily bought a curtain 2.3m long. She needed it to be 1.85m long to fit her window nicely. How many centimetres did she have to make the curtain shorter?

Answer:_____

37 $4t + 3 = 2t + 11$, What number does t stand for?

Answer:_____

38   Which one of the following ratio is equivalent to 3 : 4?

   6 : 10   4 : 20   10 : 16   9 : 14   27 : 36

Answer:_____

39   A bag has red, green and blue marbles. $\frac{1}{5}$ of them are green. $\frac{3}{5}$ of them are blue. What percentage is red?

Answer:_____

40

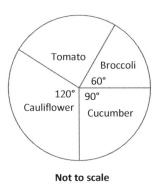

Not to scale

The pie chart shows a survey about the favourite vegetable. If 240 people were asked, how many people said Tomato?

Answer:_____

41   Tom went on an air boat ride to see alligators. It left at 09:25 and came back at 13:40. How long was the boat trip? Give your answer in hours.

Answer:_____

42   Find two whole numbers between 0 and 10 that have a sum of 13 and a product of 42.

Answer:_____, _____

43   Alex won twice as many stickers as James in school this year. They won 51 stickers altogether. How many did Alex win?

Answer:_____

44   What is the range of the following data? Give your answer in metres.

   $2.03m$ $92cm$ $4.08m$ $425mm$ $127mm$

Answer:_____

45   What is the order of rotational symmetry of a regular hexagon?

Answer:_____

46   What number is missing from the following calculation?

$36 + 75 =$_____ $+28$

Answer:_____

47   How many minutes are there in $5\frac{1}{4}$ hours?

Answer:_____

---

48   One box can hold 30 books. How many boxes do you need if you to store 520 books?

Answer:_____

49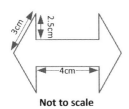

Not to scale

What is the perimeter of the shape on the left?

Answer:_____

---

50   What is the median of this set of numbers?

3   8   2   3   13   10   9   6

Answer:_____

11+ Maths

Standard Practice Paper
Pack Two 11C

Fill in your details:

Name..

Date of birth...

Male ☐   Female ☐

School..

Today's date..

Read these instructions before you start:

- You have **50 minutes** to complete this paper.
- There are **50 questions** in this paper and each question is worth one mark.
- Show all working using the space around the questions. You may receive marks for correct working even if your final answer is wrong.
- Make sure you write the answers very clearly.
- You will not lose marks for crossing out.
- Work as quickly and carefully as you can.
- If you find a question difficult, do **NOT** spend too much time on it but move on to the next one.
- **Calculators and protractors are not allowed.**

Moon Tuition
making the most of your potential

www.moontuition.co.uk

1   Complete the number sequence.

   1   8   27   _____   125

   Answer:_____

2   What symbol $(+, -, \times, \div)$ is missing from this calculation?

   8____9 + 8 = 80

   Answer:_____

3   Which of the following numbers is both a square number and a cube number?

   36   27   64   81   25   49

   Answer:_____

4   Write the inverse calculation for $12 \times 11 = 132$

   Answer:_____

5   Use the following information in the table to find the cost of 4 tickets to a theme park.

no. of tickets	1	2	3	4
total price	£9	£18	£27	

   Answer:_____

6   Jim is facing South. He turns anticlockwise 45°, then 120°and then 55°. How many more degrees does he need to turn to so that he will face South again?

   Answer:_____

7 　　Tom drew a shape. It had 4 right angles and an order of rotational symmetry of 2. What shape did he draw?

　　　　Answer:_____

8 　　　　What 3-D shape does this net make?

　　　　　　　　　　　　　　　Answer:_____

9 　　What is the answer to 12000 ÷ 30?

　　　　Answer:_____

10 　The table below shows the number of cups of tea sold in a coffee shop.

	Monday	Tuesday	Wednesday	Thursday	Friday
Tea Sold	20	32	18	35	45

What is the median number of cups of tea sold?

　　　　Answer:_____

11

What is the number indicated by the arrow?

　　　　　　　　　　　　　　Answer:_____

12   What is the biggest prime number less than 100?

Answer:_____

---

13   Put the following numbers in order, starting with the smallest.

0.3 $\frac{1}{5}$ 25% $1\frac{1}{4}$ 0.09

Answer:_____

---

14   Ollie cycles 4 times a week. How many miles does he cycle in total every week?

	Wednesday	Friday	Saturday	Sunday
Distance	6.4km	7.8km	18.5km	15.3km

Answer:_____

---

15   A small cake costs 24p and a big cake costs £1.20. I bought eight small cakes and two big cakes. How much change did I get from £10?

Answer:_____

---

16   A TV costs £600 in a shop. There is 25% discount if you order on line. How much do you need to pay if you order on line?

Answer:_____

---

17   What is the missing number in the number sequence below?

5.242   5.244   5.246   5.248   _____

Answer:_____

18   Amy is going to cook a duck weighing 2.5kg. For every kilogram of the duck, it must be cooked for 40 minutes. How many minutes does it take Amy to cook this duck?

Answer:_____

19

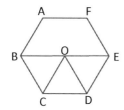

If the area of the regular hexagon is 48cm^2, what is the area of the triangle OCD?

Answer:_____

20   Mark is 92cm tall. He needs to be 1.40m tall to get on the roller coaster ride. How much taller does he need to be so that he can get on the ride?

Answer:_____

21   The length of the shorter side of a parallelogram is 12cm. Two adjacent sides are both 1.5 times longer. Work out the perimeter of this parallelogram.

Answer:_____

22

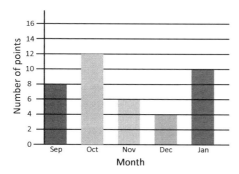

This bar chart shows the number of points scored by a team in the monthly chess club race. What is the mean number of points scored?

Answer:_____

23 $x = ab - 12$. If a=7 and b=8, what is the value of x?

Answer:_____

---

24   What is the highest common factor of 36 and 24?

Answer:_____

---

25   What is the lowest common multiple of 12 and 20?

Answer:_____

---

26   What is answer to the calculation below?

$5 + 25 \div 5 =$

Answer:_____

---

27   Ian swam $1.2km$ on Saturday. He swam 40% further on Sunday. How far did he swim on Sunday?

Answer:_____

28

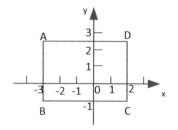

What are the coordinates of point A?

Answer:_____

29   Write the decimal 0.32 as a fraction. Leave your answer in its simplest term.

Answer:_____

30   What is the mode of the sizes of angles?

20°   45°   30°   80°   30°   120°   70°   120°

Answer:_____

31   Ian won 4 out of 6 badminton games that he played with Jim. Based on these results, how many more games do you think Ian will win if he plays 18 more games?

Answer:_____

32   Tom has 4 more PS3 games than Richard.   If Richard has x PS3 games, what expression shows the number of PS3 games Tom has?

Answer:_____

33   Granny needs to pour 4.2l water into 6 bottles evenly. How many millilitres will each bottle contain?

Answer:_____

34 If one pizza can be cut into 12 equal slices, how many whole pizzas do you have to buy if you need to have 40 slices for a party?

Answer:_____

35 Lucy is making a cake. For every 500*g* of flour, she needs to add 50*ml* of milk and 150*ml* of water. If she is using 2*kg* of flour, how many litres of water does she need to add?

Answer:_____

36 Put the following numbers in order, starting with the biggest.

3.25 $4\frac{7}{10}$ 4.09 $3\frac{3}{4}$ 1.99

Answer:_____

37 The table below shows how many meals the dinner lady sold on five days and how much money she collected. How much more money did she collect on the day she sold the most meals than the day she sold the least meal?

	meals sold	money collected
Monday	30	£84
Tuesday	35	£108
Wednesday	28	£96
Thursday	31	£93
Friday	38	£112

Answer:_____

38

2p coins

5p coins

Each jug contains only one type of coins and each of these jugs contain the same amount of money which is £2.40. How many more coins in 2p coin jug than 5p coin jug?

Answer:_____

39 Tom has 20 pens. Lucy has 13 pens. Tom gives $\frac{2}{5}$ of his pens to Lucy. How many pens do Tom and Lucy each have now?

Answer: Tom:_____, Lucy:_____

40 Richard is t years old. His sister Emily is twice as old as him. How old will Emily be in 10 years' time?

Answer:_____

41 The pattern below contains numbered shapes. What is the number in the fourth right angle triangle in this repeating pattern?

1 2 3 4 5 6 7 8

Answer:_____

© Moon Tuition
www.moontuition.co.uk

42 Ian has some bricks. Each brick is 15*cm* long. He wants to build a line of bricks that is 1.65*m* long. How many bricks does he need?

Answer:_____

43 A bottle contains 2*l* of orange juice. Patrick wants to fill 8 glasses with orange juice. Each glass can only hold 200*ml* of orange juice. How much orange juice will be left in the bottle?

Answer:_____

44 The following table shows the times in a 200*m* swimming race. What is the range of the times? Give your answer in seconds.

	200m race
Team A	1 minute 14 seconds
Team B	1 minute 08 seconds
Team C	58 seconds
Team D	56 seconds
Team E	1 minute 09 seconds

Answer:_____

45 What is the missing number in the sequence below?

1.5   2.1   3.6   5.7   _____   15

Answer:_____

46

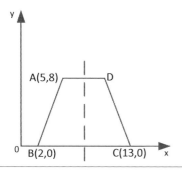

The trapezium is symmetrical. What are the coordinates of point D?

Answer:_____

47   Three-quarters of a number is 270. What is this number?

Answer:_____

48   A group of 40 people are going on a boat trip. It costs £10 per adult and £5 per child. If 40 people pay £360 altogether, how many adults are there in the group?

Answer:_____

49   Granny is making a cake. She adds $40ml$ of milk for every $500g$ of flour used. If she makes a cake with $1.5kg$ of flour, how much milk does she need to add?

Answer:_____

50

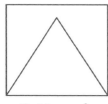

Not to scale

An equilateral triangle is inside a square. If the area of the square is $49cm^2$, what is the perimeter of the triangle?

Answer:_____

11+ Maths

Standard Practice Paper
Pack Two 11D

Fill in your details:

Name..

Date of birth...

Male ☐   Female ☐

School...

Today's date...

Read these instructions before you start:

- You have **50 minutes** to complete this paper.
- There are **50 questions** in this paper and each question is worth one mark.
- Show all working using the space around the questions. You may receive marks for correct working even if your final answer is wrong.
- Make sure you write the answers very clearly.
- You will not lose marks for crossing out.
- Work as quickly and carefully as you can.
- If you find a question difficult, do **NOT** spend too much time on it but move on to the next one.
- **Calculators and protractors are not allowed.**

Moon Tuition
making the most of your potential

www.moontuition.co.uk

1   Write these prices in order, starting with the highest.

£3.08   38p   £3.80   £3.09   £0.99   £2.99

Answer:_____

---

2   Liam has a packet of marbles: 3 red, 4 blue and 5 yellow. What is the probability of picking a blue marble? Give your answer as a fraction.

Answer:_____

---

3   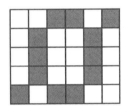   What percentage of the shape is unshaded?

Answer:_____

---

4   Charlie thinks of a number. He multiplies it by 6 and then adds 9 to the result. His answer is 51. What number did he think of?

Answer:_____

---

5   Calculate $\frac{5}{12}$ of 132.

Answer:_____

---

6   Richard rides his bike to his school every morning because his school is only 2 miles away. His average cycling speed is $6 miles/hour$. How long does it take him to get to his school every morning?

Answer:_____

7   *m* stands for a number. Write the expression of 6 more than half m.

Answer:_____

---

8   The table below shows the number of red and green apples in bag A and bag B. Tom chooses an apple from each bag without looking. From which bag is he more likely to choose green apples?

	red apples	green apples
bag A	4	6
bag B	3	9

Answer:_____

9

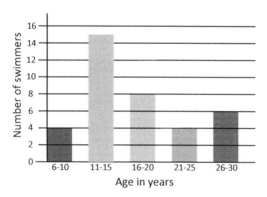

This graph shows the age of the swimmers in a swimming club. How many swimmers are aged 20 or younger?

Answer:_____

---

10   All prime numbers are odd numbers. Is this statement TRUE or FALSE?

Answer:_____

11   Lisa drew a quadrilateral. It has 4 equal sides and two acute angles. What shape did she draw?

Answer:_____

12   Which two decimals have a difference of 0.4?

0.25   0.75   1.05   0.70   1.15

Answer:_____

13

Ollie has three marbles which weigh 600g in total. Marble A and B together weigh the same as Marble C. Marble A weighs one third of Marble C. How much does Marble B weigh?

Answer:_____

14   Write all the prime numbers between 1 and 20.

Answer:_____

15   Convert 24% to a fraction. Give your answer in the simplest term.

Answer:_____

16

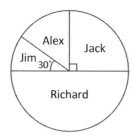

Seventy two students took a prediction survey about who would win the chess game. How many students predicted Alex would win?

Answer:_____

17

Round $6\frac{4}{5}$ to the nearest whole number.

Answer:_____

18

A4 size envelops are sold in a pack of 20. John needs 116 A4 size envelops. How many packs does he have to buy?

Answer:_____

19

William has a bag which contains 4 apples and 6 bananas only. He puts 1 more apple and 4 more bananas in the bag. What fraction of the fruits in the bag are bananas now? Give the answer in its simplest term.

Answer:_____

20

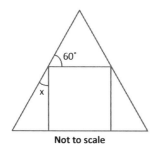

Not to scale

Inside the triangle, there is a square. Calculate the size of angle x in the diagram.

Answer:_____

21

Recipe
200*ml* of milk
1*kg* of flour
4 tea spoons of sugar

Amy uses this recipe to make a cake. How many tea spoons of sugar does she need if she uses 750*g* of flour?

Answer:_____

---

22   There are 32 children in the class. Each needs 2 bottles of water for a school trip. Bottles of water are sold in packs of 12. How many packs need to be bought?

Answer:_____

---

23   Jack, Patrick and Richard ran a 100*m* race. Richard finished 2 seconds before Patrick. Jack finished 3 seconds after Patrick. Richard's time was 12 seconds. What was Jack's time in seconds?

Answer:_____

---

24   Amy and Kate had £2.50 altogether. Kate gave 20p to Amy so that both have the same amount. How much money did Amy have at the start?

Answer:_____

---

25   Work out 0.4×0.25

Answer:_____

26   Ian scored 57 out 60 in a Non-Verbal Reasoning practice test. What percentage did he score?

Answer:_____

27   The cost for taking a taxi is £1.20 per mile. Four people take a taxi to the airport which is 20 miles away. They share the cost equally. How much does each of them pay?

Answer:_____

28

Jonathan has a jug with concentrated apple juice in it. The level of the juice is shown in the diagram. He adds 0.12l of water in the jug to dilute the apple juice. What is the new level of the juice? Draw a line to show your answer.

Answer:_____

29   Calculate 0.56×2.5

Answer:_____

30   Tom bought two muffins and one mug of hot chocolate. He paid £4.20. Charlie bought one muffin and one mug of hot chocolate. He paid £2.70. Work out the cost of hot chocolate.

Answer:_____

31

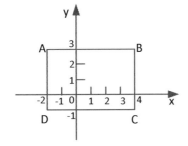

Here is a rectangle on x and y axes. Calculate the perimeter of this rectangle.

Answer:_____

32

Find a number which fits all of the following three statements:

It is a multiple of 3.
It is a multiple of 4.
It is bigger than 40 and smaller than 50.

Answer:_____

33

A book shop has a promotion: Buy Three Get the Cheapest One Half Price. Amy wants to buy three books which cost £9.99, £4.98 and £3.60. How much does she need to pay if she buys all three books?

Answer:_____

34

How many vertices does a cuboid have?

Answer:_____

35

A school sells the concert tickets for a charity. For each ticket sold, £1.50 is given to the charity. If the charity got £30, how many tickets were sold?

Answer:_____

36   How many quarters are there in 12?

Answer:_____

37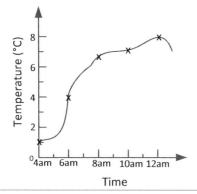

This graph shows the temperature of a winter morning in London. Use this graph to find the range of the temperature.

Answer:_____

38   Round 349.578 to the nearest whole number.

Answer:_____

39   Granny needs 1.2kg of potatoes to make a dish. She has 400g of potatoes already on the weighing scale. How many more grams of potatoes need to be added to the scale?

Answer:_____

40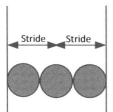

Two strides have the same length as three footballs. How many footballs will have the same length as one hundred strides.

Answer:_____

41   What is 30% of 140?

Answer:_____

---

42   Round 3.0564 to 2 decimal places.

Answer:_____

43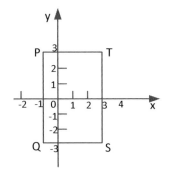

PQST is a rectangle. Is point W with coordinates (-1.5, 2) inside the rectangle or outside?

Answer:_____

---

44   Mike is y years old. His sister is 5 years younger than him. How old will his sister be in 10 years' time?

Answer:_____

---

45   Round 14.348 to the nearest hundredth.

Answer:_____

---

46 $3a - 4 = a + 7$
Work out the value of a.

Answer:_____

47

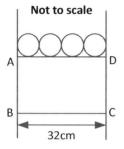

Not to scale

A   D

B   C

32cm

The diagram shows the rectangle ABCD which has the same length as 4 circles. If BC=32cm, calculate the radius of the circle.

Answer:_____

48

06:15	Music
07:00	News
07:20	Weather Report
07:30	Sports News

The table above shows the radio programmes in one evening. Tom turns on the radio at 06:52. How long does he have to wait for the Sports News?

Answer:_____

49

If Tom swims for n minutes every day, how many hours does he swim for one week including weekends?

Answer:_____

50

The table below shows the prices of two items. Work out the price of the dining table.

	Price
Sofa and Dining Table	£400
Dining Table and Chairs	£200
Sofa and Chairs	£300

Answer:_____

11+ Maths

Answer Key for
Standard Practice Papers
Pack Two

Read these instructions before you start marking:

- Only the answers given are allowed.
- One mark should be given for each correct answer.
- Half mark can be given for correct working if the final answer is wrong.
- Do not deduct marks for the wrong answers.

Moon Tuition

making the most of your potential

www.moontuition.co.uk

Practice Paper 11A

1.	4634	26.	30*cm*
2.	896	27.	£640
3.	672	28.	25% or $\frac{1}{4}$
4.	863	29.	11
5.	301407	30.	79
6.	18.4	31.	180
7.	2120	32.	1983
8.	7	33.	110.7
9.	20	34.	16
10.	£4.30	35.	6.3*m*
11.	1.35 0.41 0.27 0.23 0.09	36.	3.65*l*
12.	20000	37.	80*cm*^{2}
13.	243.6	38.	£18.62
14.	54	39.	C
15.	96	40.	6 minutes
16.	64	41.	20
17.	24	42.	49*km*
18.	80	43.	8
19.	4	44.	105
20.	3.5	45.	2
21.	7.4	46.	(3,7)
22.	4 days	47.	£30
23.	8	48.	102 *km/hr*
24.	43.8*kg*	49.	£1440
25.	£150	50.	30

Practice Paper 11B

1.	5	26.	$\frac{10}{16}$
2.	120	27.	4
3.	5.1	28.	49
4.	$\frac{12}{25}$	29.	cube
5.	3, 5 and 37	30.	75
6.	$x = 53$; $y = 21$	31.	25%
7.	9	32.	$1.2kg$
8.	-2°C	33.	$0.2l$
9.	£3.80	34.	29
10.	Alex is taller by 10 cm.	35.	45
11.	£21.6	36.	$45cm$
12.	51, 234, 81	37.	4
13.	1.30	38.	$27 : 36$
14.	12.5%	39.	20%
15.	14:45 or 2:45pm	40.	60
16.	43.95	41.	$4\frac{1}{4}$ hours or 4.25hours
17.	48p	42.	6 and 7
18.	$24cm^2$	43.	34
19.	48	44.	$3.953m$
20.	90	45.	6
21.	8	46.	83
22.	TRUE, 121 is 11^2.	47.	315
23.	x=60°, y=120°	48.	18
24.	6 hours	49.	$30cm$
25.	£9.06, £8.60, £8.09, £0.99, 96p	50.	7

Practice Paper 11C

1.	64	26.	10
2.	×	27.	$1.68km$
3.	64	28.	(-3, 2.5)
4.	$132 \div 12 = 11$ or $132 \div 11 = 12$	29.	$\frac{8}{25}$
5.	£36	30.	30° and 120°
6.	140°	31.	12
7.	rectangle	32.	$x + 4$
8.	square based pyramid	33.	$700ml$
9.	400	34.	4
10.	32	35.	$0.6l$
11.	-0.4	36.	$4\frac{7}{10}$, 4.09, $3\frac{3}{4}$, 3.25, 1.99
12.	97	37.	£16
13.	0.09, $\frac{1}{5}$, 25%, 0.3, $1\frac{1}{4}$	38.	72
14.	30 miles	39.	Tom: 12, Lucy:21
15.	£5.68	40.	$2t + 10$
16.	£450	41.	14
17.	5.25	42.	11
18.	100 minutes	43.	$0.4l$ or $400ml$
19.	$8cm^2$	44.	18
20.	$48cm$	45.	9.3
21.	$60cm$	46.	D(10, 8)
22.	8	47.	360
23.	44	48.	32
24.	12	49.	$120ml$
25.	60	50.	$21cm$

Practice Paper 11D

1.	£3.80, £3.09, £3.08, £2.99, £0.99, 38p	26.	95%
2.	$\frac{1}{3}$ or $\frac{4}{12}$	27.	£6
3.	60%	28.	$160ml$
4.	7	29.	1.4
5.	55	30.	£1.20
6.	20 minutes	31.	20
7.	$6 + \frac{1}{2}m$	32.	48
8.	bag B	33.	£16.77
9.	27	34.	8
10.	FALSE (2 is a prime number)	35.	20
11.	Rhombus	36.	48
12.	0.75 and 1.15	37.	7°C
13.	$200g$	38.	350
14.	2, 3, 5, 7, 11, 13, 17, 19	39.	$800g$
15.	$\frac{6}{25}$	40.	150
16.	12	41.	42
17.	7	42.	3.06
18.	6	43.	Outside
19.	$\frac{2}{3}$	44.	$y + 5$
20.	30°	45.	14.35
21.	3	46.	5.5
22.	6	47.	$4cm$
23.	17s	48.	38 minutes
24.	£1.05	49.	$\frac{7}{60}n$
25.	0.1	50.	£150

Printed in Great Britain
by Amazon